DEC 2005

LI

SCIENCE VIEW

ELECTRICITY & MAGNETISM

©2005 by Chelsea House Publishers, a subsidiary of Haights Cross Communications.

A Haights Cross Communications ✦ Company

Printed and bound in China.
10 9 8 7 6 5 4 3 2 1

Library of Congress Cataloging-in-Publication Data applied for.

ISBN: 0-7910-8208-3

Chelsea House Publishers

2080 Cabot Blvd. West, Suite 201
Langhorne, PA 19047-1813

http://www.chelseahouse.com

Produced by

David West 👫 **Children's Books**
7 Princeton Court
55 Felsham Road
London SW15 1AZ

Designer: Rob Shone
Editor: Gail Bushnell
Picture Research: Carlotta Cooper

An explanation of difficult words can be found in the glossary on page 31.

SCIENCE VIEW

ELECTRICITY & MAGNETISM

Steve Parker

CHELSEA HOUSE
PUBLISHERS
A Haights Cross Communications Company

CONTENTS

WARNING! All projects should be supervised by a responsible adult. Some need extra care and expert help, and are marked with a red box. Make sure the instructions are followed. *Never take risks.*

INTRODUCTION

What do a light bulb, a refrigerator magnet, a medical scanner that looks inside the body, and a vacuum cleaner have in common? They all work by electricity, or magnetism, or both—using one of the most basic forces in the whole universe. Without them, modern life would come to a cold dark halt.

How it WORKS

These panels explain the science behind the projects, and the processes and principles that we see every day, but which we may not always understand!

PROJECTS

The projects are simple to do with supervision, using household items. Remember— scientists are cautious. They prepare equipment thoroughly, they know what should happen, and they *always* put safety first.

Static electricity (electrostatic charge) builds up in clouds until it is powerful enough to leap to the ground as a flash of lightning.

Electricity creates giant lightning bolts and powers huge machines, but it is based on some of the tiniest particles of all–electrons.

ALL THINGS ARE ATOMS

Everything in the universe, from a speck of dust to massive stars deep in space, is made of tiny pieces called atoms. They are so small, this period contains millions of them.

COLLECT STATIC

Polystyrene cup "handle" glued to dish

Metal foil dish

Polystyrene plate

Small water-filled plastic casing

Metal foil

Nail

Spark

Wires

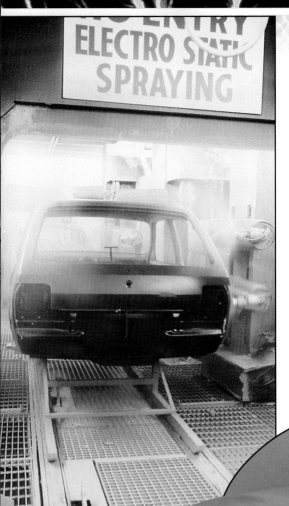

Substances with opposite static charges attract. If the car is positive and the paint negative, the paint sticks better.

Electrons on the Go = Electricity

Inside an atom, particles called protons and neutrons clump in a central nucleus, and around this whiz yet more particles– electrons. Rubbing a substance can cause electrons to detach from their atoms, ready to "jump" to other atoms. This is static electricity, or electric charge. Billions of electrons all "hopping" steadily from atom to atom, in the same direction, form the flow of energy we call electric current.

Animal muscles give out tiny electrical pulses that pass through water. A shark can detect them to find its prey.

A capacitor stores static or electric charge. Make one as shown at left.

Rub wool on the polystyrene plate for a minute, then touch it to the dish. Hold the dish by its "handle" and touch it briefly to the foil and nail. Bring the wires together. Watch for a spark.

WARNING: Charging the capacitor more than four times can store enough static electricity to give a small shock if you touch the foil and nail. Handle with care.

How it WORKS

Rubbing the plate makes electrons come away from their atoms, forming static charge. The charge passes to the metal foil dish when touched, and then to the nail and water in the plastic casing. When wires link the foil and nail, the charge evens out with a tiny spark.

Nucleus

Spark

Positive charge

Negative charge

Electrons

Magnetism is very mysterious. This invisible force affects only certain substances, and, like electricity, it comes from the tiniest parts of atoms– electrons.

IN A SPIN

Electricity is due to the movement of "free" electrons jumping from atom to atom. Magnetism is due to the way electrons spin around like tiny tops, as they swirl about inside their atoms. If the spinning directions of all the electrons in billions of atoms line up in a certain way, the result is a magnetic force that can push, pull, twist, and turn.

This magnetic resonance imaging scanner uses a powerful magnetic field. The resulting MRI scan gives the doctor a picture of the patient's insides.

Magnetism is strong enough to make an entire train "float" above the rails, without wheels. This is maglev, or magnetic levitation.

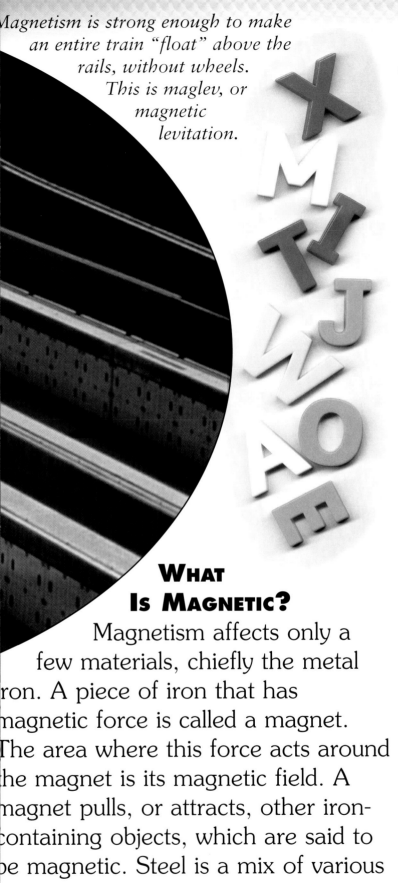

Magnets can hold letters on metal surfaces, such as refrigerators (left). Each letter has a disk magnet, which has a pole on each side.

Different shapes do different jobs. Ring magnets have poles on the inner and outer rings. Horseshoes have a pole at each end.

WHAT IS MAGNETIC?

Magnetism affects only a few materials, chiefly the metal iron. A piece of iron that has magnetic force is called a magnet. The area where this force acts around the magnet is its magnetic field. A magnet pulls, or attracts, other iron-containing objects, which are said to be magnetic. Steel is a mix of various substances, mainly iron, so steel is magnetic, too.

How it WORKS

A magnet's field is strongest in two places called poles. These have opposing forces to each other, called North (N or +), and South (S or -). With two magnets, poles of the same kind push apart, or repel. Poles of opposite kinds pull together, or attract.

Opposite poles attract

Like poles repel

We cannot see magnetic force, which is just as well, because it is all around us. The Earth is a giant magnet, whose magnetism has long been used by people.

The Sun's "solar wind" consists of billions of tiny electrically charged particles. They hit Earth's magnetism high above and glow as auroras (northern and southern lights).

THE SPINNING CORE

Deep inside the Earth is the planet's core, a vast ball of red-hot, iron-rich rocks. The rock is heated so much, it can flow like molasses. As the Earth spins around daily, the core swirls around, too, and makes magnetism.

POINTING TO THE POLES

Water-filled shallow dish

Slice of cork

Magnetized needle

Painted cardboard disk

FINDING THE WAY

A compass is a long, slim magnet, often shaped like a needle, which can turn or swivel easily. Due to attraction and repulsion, its own poles swing around to line up with the Earth's magnetic force, and point to the magnetic North and South Poles.

Migrating whales, fish, and birds like these stilts may find their way using Earth's magnetic field.

VERY USEFUL

People have used compasses to navigate across land and sea for a thousand years. Some animals have a "natural compass" in their bodies to find their way on migration.

A magnetic compass is used to position the map correctly as people travel through the wilderness.

A steel needle stroked the same way 20-plus times with the same end of a magnet becomes a magnet itself.

Put it on a slice of floating cork. It always points the same way.

How it **WORKS**

The magnetized needle works like a compass, being affected by the magnetic field surrounding Earth. The field is made of invisible lines of magnetic force. One end of the compass is attracted to the planet's North Pole and the other to the South Pole.

Magnetic North Pole

Earth's lines of magnetic force

Compasses align with magnetic field

Magnetic South Pole

11

Massive electromagnets in ironworks, steel factories, and scrap yards can lift magnetic objects weighing many tons. Non-magnetic (non-iron) materials are left behind–a useful way of sorting scrap metals for recycling.

Wherever there is electricity, there's also magnetism. An electric current flowing through a wire makes a magnetic field around the wire. This is the electromagnetic effect.

A loudspeaker has both kinds of magnets. Electric signals in the electromagnet make it push and pull against th magnet, moving the speaker cone

ON AND OFF

If the current-carrying wire is looped into a coil around an iron rod or bar, called the core, this makes its magnetism much stronger. The resulting device is known as an electromagnet. The magnetism of an electromagnet is the same as the magnetism from a magnet, except for one feature. If an electromagnet's current is turned off, its magnetism disappears.

MAKE AN ELECTROMAGNET

Magnetic objects

Wire coil

Metal nail

Battery

PULLING POWER

A solenoid is similar to an electromagnet. It has a movable iron core at one end of the coil. Turning it on makes the core slide quickly into the center of the coil. Turning it off allows a spring to pull the core back again.

Electromagnets in "tube"-type televisions move the beam of electrons that builds up the picture on screen.

Wires buried in floors and roads have magnetic fields around them. These can be detected and followed by robot transporters in factories.

EVERYDAY HELPERS

We use electromagnets and solenoids many times daily, without realizing it. They are found in loudspeakers, doorbells, and the sliding bolts in remote-control security locks on cars and house doors.

A large iron nail and plastic-coated wire make a simple electromagnet.

Wind the wire tightly at least 20 times round the nail–more turns make stronger magnetism. Connect the wire's ends to a battery–more volts make more magnetism–so try a 9-volt battery. The electromagnet will attract magnetic objects.

How it **WORKS**

Most iron-based substances have tiny areas of magnetism called domains. Normally, these are all mixed up, pointing in different directions, so they cancel out. A nearby electric current makes the domains point in the same direction, so their magnetism adds up to make a strong magnetic field.

1   **2**

S Circuit of electricity

N Nail becomes magnet with poles

Electricity changes the tiny domains from random (1) to aligned (2).

Electricity produces magnetism, in an electromagnet–and the opposite is true. Magnetism can make electricity. This effect also occurs many times in daily life.

MOVING OR CHANGING

When a wire and magnet move in relation to each other, electricity flows in the wire. This is known as electromagnetic (EM) induction. It does not matter if the wire stays still and the magnetic field around it moves, or if the field is still and the wire moves–electric current is still induced.

In some trains, diesel engines drive generators that make electricity for motors. Both the generators and motors work using electromagnetic induction.

A metal-detector makes a magnetic field around itself. An iron-based object distorts the field, triggering the sensor.

electromagnet
s switched on
y current

Link wires

Coil

Wire
holder

Windmill

Magnet

Compass moves when
current flows

CHANGING STRENGTH

Even if the magnetic
field and the wire stay
till, electricity can still
be induced. This
happens if the field
changes in strength,
becoming more or
ess powerful.

INDUCTION
EVERYWHERE

EM induction is used
n all kinds of devices,
rom electric guitars to
raffic lights. With its
"opposite," the electromagnetic effect, it
s vital in machines such as generators
nd motors, as will be seen later.

Make a small electric
current using wind.

Push paperclip
wire holders
into a paper cup
and position
magnet. Make a
wire coil. Scrape
the insulation off
one side of each end
of the coil wire (see
close-up on page 25).
Thread the ends
through the holders.
Fix a windmill to one
end. Connect link
wires to the holders
(inside cup) and then
to the electromagnet
(see page 12).

*Wind turbines are
another form of
generator. However,
they use natural
power as an
energy source.*

How it WORKS

When the wind blows, the
compass moves! As the coil turns
near the magnet, an induced
current flows around the coil. It
flows down one wire holder and
link wire to the electromagnet, and
then back to the coil. The
electromagnet's field attracts the
magnetic compass. A rule describes
this movement.

RIGHT-HAND RULE

Movement of coil (thumb)

Direction of
magnetic field
(first finger)

Direction of current
(second finger)

The "right-hand rule"
shows the current's
direction according to
the magnetic field and
coil motion.

*A guitar's strings move in the
magnetism of the pickup, creating
electricity in the pickup's wire coil.*

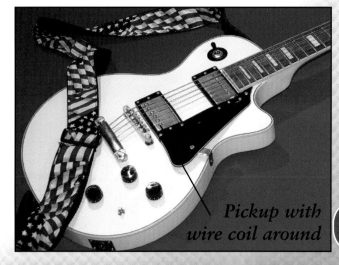

*Pickup with
wire coil around*

15

Electrical energy is so useful because it can be made from many other kinds of energy–and changed back into them, too.

A control room engineer checks the amount of electricity being produced in a power station.

SOURCES OF ELECTRICITY

Many energy forms can be converted directly into electric current, including chemicals, heat, movement, and light. There are chemicals inside batteries and the fuels burned in power stations, heat and movement can be found in power station generators, and light for solar panels and small solar cells is used in calculators.

How it WORKS

There are many designs of battery, but a typical version has two metallic electrodes–anode (+) and cathode (-). There is a paste or powder electrolyte between them. Chemical changes between electrodes and electrolyte make electrons leave their atoms and flow out from the negative contact along a wire, back to the positive

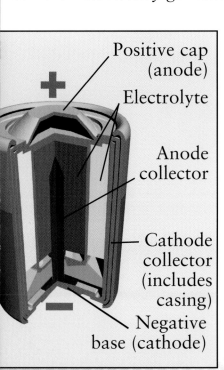

ALTERNATE OR DIRECT?

The way power station generators work means their electricity flows one way, then the other, and so on–reversing itself 50 to 60 times each second. This type of flow is known as alternating current, AC. Batteries (electrical cells) make a steady one-way flow of electricity called direct current, DC.

Water piled up behind a hydro-electric dam flows along pipes to an-like turbines in huge casings, which turn electricity generators.

Solar panels have thousands of button-sized photovoltaic cells. The Sun's light energy knocks electrons from their atoms to make the electric current.

Positive cap (anode)

Electrolyte

Anode collector

Cathode collector (includes casing)

Negative base (cathode)

INSIDE A BATTERY

Batteries are convenient "packages" of chemicals that react together to make electrons come away from their atoms. This only happens when the battery is linked by wires to an electrical device, and the electrons have somewhere to flow. Otherwise, there is no reaction.

A rechargeable battery uses the electricity put in to reverse the chemical reactions, so it can give out electricity again.

17

ROUND AND ROUND

Electricity does not flow unless it has somewhere to go. Usually, this is around a continuous pathway from its source, out and back again.

CIRCUITS

Electricity's pathway is known as a circuit. Parts of the circuit are metal wires, which carry electricity well. The circuit can also include useful components, such as a small light bulb or a huge electric motor. The current flowing through these components makes them work.

Railroad power lines carry current many miles, with the train motors as part of the very long circuit.

MAKE A CIRCUIT BOARD

Switches

Connecting wire

Battery

Light bulb

You can make a circuit board with several paths for a battery's electricity, through wires and bulbs. Switches can be made with paperclips between gaps in the wire circuit. By using the switches to connect to different parts of the circuit, you can make either the bulbs on the left, or those on the right, light up. Which ones are the brightest?

How it WORKS

In a series circuit (1), electricity flows through each component in turn. Its "push" in volts is shared, and so the bulbs glow dimmer. In a parallel circuit (2), current flows at full power through all components, and so the bulbs glow brighter.

n some circuits, wires are replaced by metal strips on a heet-like board. These circuit boards are found in many lectrical appliances, such as televisions and computers.

1 Series circuit

Parallel circuit

Wires carrying huge amounts of electricity in factories are usually protected from damage by tubes known as conduits.

ON AND OFF

Most circuits contain a component known as a switch. When this is "on," it makes a path for electricity and allows it to flow around the complete circuit. Turn it "off" and it makes a small break or gap. Electricity cannot pass through the air in the gap, and so it stops.

MANY PATHWAYS

Simple circuits, like those in flashlights and toys, have just one pathway for electricity. Others have hundreds of wires and other connectors and thousands of components. The current is shared between the components depending on how they are joined.

A car's spark plug has a tiny gap at the bottom. However, the electricity is powerful enough (in volts) to leap across this as a spark.

19

Electricity travels huge distances to our homes, schools, offices, and factories. Making it and distributing it are massive industries.

Power stations run day and night to keep up supplies.

VOLTAGE

Electricity is measured in various ways. Its force or pushing strength is measured in volts. A flashlight battery produces just a few volts. Car batteries are usually 12 or 24 volts. The mainline electricity from wall sockets is 240 volts–which is strong enough to kill. In big overhead power lines, the electricity may be 400,000 volts or more–enough to supply thousands of homes.

Electricity enters a building through a consumer unit. This has circuit breakers to switch off the current if there is a fault.

MAKE A DIMMER SWITCH

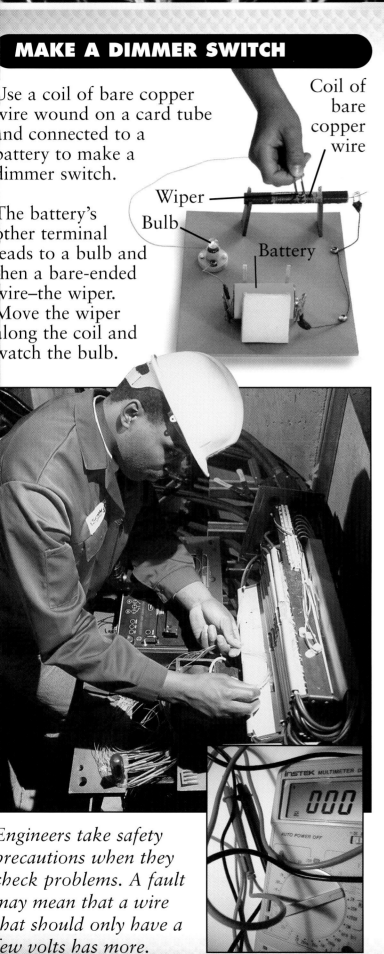

Use a coil of bare copper wire wound on a card tube and connected to a battery to make a dimmer switch.

The battery's other terminal leads to a bulb and then a bare-ended wire–the wiper. Move the wiper along the coil and watch the bulb.

Coil of bare copper wire

Wiper

Bulb

Battery

Engineers take safety precautions when they check problems. A fault may mean that a wire that should only have a few volts has more.

How it WORKS

Moving the wiper along the coil changes the length of copper wire in the circuit. The greater the length of wire, the greater its resistance. With more wire, less electricity flows around the circuit, and so the bulb gradually glows less brightly.

High resistance

Low resistance

RESIST THE FLOW

Amps (amperes) show the quantity or amount of current. One amp is over 6 septillion (6 + 24 zeros) electrons per second! Ohms measure resistance–how easily a substance or object carries electric current. As the resistance goes up, the electricity passing through goes down.

WHAT'S A WATT?

The rate at which energy is used or changed is known in science as power, and is measured in watts. Electricity is energy, and so its use is counted in watts. In an electrical circuit, the number of watts equals the volts multiplied by the amps.

The multimeter is adjusted to measure volts (V), amps (A), ohms (Ω), or other units.

21

We usually join electrical parts like bulbs and batteries with wires. Why? Because the metal of a wire carries electricity well–it is a good conductor.

EASY FLOW

Nearly all metals are good conductors. One of the best is silver. Yet it is too costly for general use, apart from special equipment such as certain computer parts. One of the next best is copper, which is cheaper, and is used for wires in homes and buildings.

A lightning conductor is a metal strap that runs from the top of a tall building, such as the Eiffel Tower. It carries the surge of lightning safely into the ground.

Scientists are working on superconductors that will carry electricity perfectly and so save energy. Metals are put in liquid helium at very low temperatures.

Massive copper wires would be heavy and unsuitable for overhead power lines. So other metals are used, including lightweight aluminum.

No Flow

An insulator is a substance that has a very high resistance– it is very bad at carrying electricity. Examples include wood, glass, paper, cardboard, rubber, plastics, and ceramics. Semiconductors carry some electricity or not, depending on how they are used.

Materials to be tested

Terminals

Use a simple circuit to test if materials are conductors.

Touch the paperclip terminals to substances, like foil, wood, plastic, and the "lead" of a pencil. Does the bulb light?

How it WORKS

The test substance completes the electrical circuit through the bulb. If the substance is a good conductor, the maximum electricity flows and the bulb glows brightly. If it is an effective insulator, hardly any current passes and the bulb stays unlit. Semiconductors cause a faint glow. Cardboard is usually a good insulator, but try it soaked in water. Does the result mean that water is a conductor?

High-voltage wires at a power station have disk-like insulators to prevent current from leaking into the ground.

23

Great lengths of electrical wiring have been wound onto drums, by using motors to turn the drums. The wires will be wrapped into coils–for more electric motors.

One of the most useful of all machines is the motor. It changes electrical energy into the spinning movement that drives countless machines and gadgets.

ATTRACT AND REPEL

Most motors use the electromagnetic effect. Current flows through a wire coil on an axle or shaft. The coil becomes an electromagnet. Nearby is another magnet. The two magnetic fields interact, alternately attracting and repelling to make the coil spin on its shaft.

Streetcars and subway trains use electric motors. They speed up and slow down quickly and release no harmful fumes unlike gasoline or diesel engines.

ee how a motor works
by adapting the wind-
turbine (page 15).

crape the
insulation
off one
ide of
each end
of the coil
wire. Connect
he battery to the
wire holders with the
oil resting between the
holders. If the coil does
not start to spin, give it
little push. When
electrical current flows
hrough the coil, does it
move–and which way?

Wire
holder

Coil

Magnet

Link
wire

Wire
with
insulation
on one side

Battery

WARNING: Disconnect battery
after two minutes to prevent the
wire holders from getting hot.

SWITCHED AROUND

n a DC (battery) motor, for every turn
of the coil, the current is reversed and
switched back again, so the magnetic
fields push and pull at the correct times.
A rotating switch on the shaft, the
commutator, does this. Some AC motors
ack a commutator since the current
reverses itself.

ENERGY EFFICIENT

Motors change over
wo-thirds of electrical
energy into motion–
much more than gasoline
or diesel engines.

Magnets

Coils

*Motors in appliances
and tools have many
sets of coils (above) and
spin within curved magnets.*

How it WORKS

Electric current passes along
the link wires and through the
coil, making it an electromagnet
with two poles. These attract or
repel the poles of the small
magnet, depending on which
way the current flows. Using
half insulated wire makes the
current switch on and off to
keep the coil spinning. The coil's
movement is described by a rule.

LEFT-HAND RULE

Movement of coil
(thumb)

Direction of
magnetic
field (first
finger)

Direction of current
(second finger)

The "left-hand rule"
shows the motor's
motion according to
the magnetic field
and current.

On a hot summer night, people at home turn up the air conditioning, sit down to watch television, and then CLICK....

OH No!

… It's a power outage! The house goes dark and silent. Only at these times do we realize how much we rely on electricity for light, climate control, sound, vision, computers, and so on.

Night turns into day at the flick of a switch, allowing people to work or play at any hour. In cold places, heating uses far more electricity than lighting.

Massive stores are devoted to selling all kinds of electric gadgets, appliances, and tools. Electrical energy is usually quiet, clean, and efficient–but must be kept safe at all times.

COVERED WITH COPPER

WARNING: An adult should supervise this project. The materials can get hot, so handle with care.

Anode and cathode in the electrolyte.

Anode (copper)

Copper layer

Cathode after plating

Electrically powered robots replace human muscle power for many factory tasks, such as welding cars.

SPECIALIST USES

Many gadgets and appliances we buy are powered by electricity–and made by it, too. Factories are full of electric motors, drills, and other tools. One specialized method is electroplating, using electricity to cover one substance with a thin layer of another substance. Items that look valuable, as if made of "solid" gold or silver, may be ordinary metal underneath.

Electroplating covers every tiny nook and cranny, atom by atom. It can plate a cheap, dull metal with shiny chromium.

Electric cars are gradually becoming powerful and fast. A problem is the limited distance they can travel before their batteries need a recharge–which can take hours.

In electroplating, a current passes between two terminals, the positive anode and negative cathode. Try it yourself.

Use a piece of copper for the anode and steel for the cathode, with dissolved Epsom salts as the electrolyte for the current to pass through. Leave it for a day.

How it WORKS

The electricity makes atoms of copper leave the anode, when they gain a positive charge. They are then called ions. They float in the electrolyte and are drawn to the negative terminal of the cathode, where they stick tight.

Steel cathode

Copper anode

Copper atoms stick to steel

+ –

Microchips are usually smaller than a fingernail, protected in black plastic cases and joined into circuits by metal contacts around the edge.

Electronic devices make sounds and pictures, control and measure, calculate and memorize. But when does electric become electronic?

SMALLER

Size and movement are the key. A washing machine is electrical, with moving parts. The only moving parts in the electronic microchip, which controls it, are electrons.

Dozens of microchips fit onto a silicon wafer smaller than a CD.

CHIPS EVERYWHERE

Electronic devices called microchips are small slices or "chips" of a semi-conductor substance, silicon. Millions of microscopic parts and components are etched or "carved" onto the chip's surface by laser light, chemicals, and other techniques.

How it WORKS

When a microchip is made, all the components are in position, already connected together, or integrated. So, microchips are also known as ICs, or integrated circuits.

1 Silicon wafers

2 Circuits printed on wafer

3 Wafer cut into chips

4 Finished chip

The biggest computers are called mainframes. They are used for immense tasks like controlling a space mission or predicting the weather.

Faster Than Thinking

A chip's components form incredibly complex circuits that send and receive so many electrical signals, so fast, that they almost think like you do!

Older planes had electrical dials and switches. Modern planes have electronic touch screens.

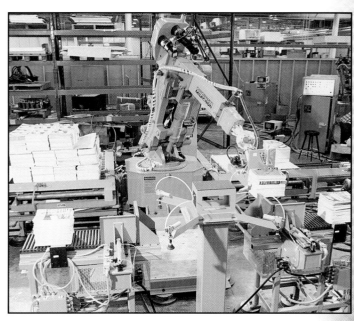

An electrical machine, like a robot, usually has an electronic microchip "brain" that tells it what to do.

VOLTS, AMPS, OHMS, AND WATTS

The volt measures the pushing strength of electricity. This is potential difference (pd), or electromotive force (emf)–see panel, right. The ampere (amp) measures the quantity of electrical charge flowing past, one amp being about 6.28 septillion electrons passing per second. The ohm is the resistance, or opposition, to this flow. These units are linked by one of the most important laws in electrical engineering, known as Ohm's law:

V (volts) = I (amps) x R (ohms)

The watt is a unit of power–that is, the rate of using or converting energy. It applies to all energy forms, but with electricity:

W (watts) = V (volts) x I (amps)

ELECTRICAL CHARGE

Electrical charge is, or is caused by, electrons separated from their atoms and ready to flow or actually moving. It is measured in coulombs. One coulomb is the amount of charge that makes up a current of one amp (see above). Capacitors store charge and are rated in farads. One farad is a store or capacitance of one coulomb per volt.

HOW MANY VOLTS?

• Major cross-country powerlines	400,000 plus
• Local power lines, railroads	33,000
• Smaller factories, workshops	440
• Mainline supply (US/UK)	220/110
• Telephone ringing signal	50–100
• Truck and tractor batteries	24
• Car batteries	12
• Portable "powerpack" battery	9
• Typical LED display	5
• Flashlight battery	1.5
• Nerve signal in human body	0.01

MAGNETIC UNITS

The strength of a magnetic field over the whole area of the field, which is like the total "quantity" of magnetism, is called magnetic flux. It is measured in webers (Wb). The strength of a magnetic field in a certain area, which is like the number of lines of magnetic force in that area, is magnetic flux density. It is measured in teslas (T). One tesla is one weber per 10.76 sq ft (1 sq m).

HOW MANY WATTS?

1000 watts would power average examples of these devices for this long:

• Instant-heat shower	5–10 minutes
• Electric kettle	30 minutes
• Microwave oven	30–60 minutes
• Standard electric heater	1 hour
• Food processor	2–3 hours
• Home computer	3–5 hours
• Big-screen television	5 hours
• Standard light bulb (100W)	10 hours
• Electric toothbrush	30-plus hours

STRENGTH OF MAGNETIC FIELD

Comparative strengths of magnetic fields, in teslas, include:

• Most powerful fields for scientific research	40
• Scrap yard magnet or medical MRI scanner	1–5
• Refrigerator magnet	0.1
• Earth's field at pole	0.00006
• Earth's field at equator	0.000025
• Nerve signals in brain	0.000000001

GLOSSARY

anode
An electrode connected to the positive terminal (+) of a battery or other electricity source.

atom
The smallest particle of an element, made up of a central nucleus surrounded by electrons.

cathode
An electrode connected to the negative terminal (-) of a battery or other electricity source.

conduction
When energy, such as heat or electricity, moves through an object or from one object to another.

current
In electricity, the quantity or amount of electrical energy, in terms of numbers of electrons. It is measured in amps.

domain
A tiny area of magnetism within a magnet.

electrode
A contact or terminal through which electricity passes in or out of a substance.

electromagnetic effect
When an electric current flows through a wire or similar conductor and creates a magnetic field around the wire.

electromagnetic induction
When a wire or similar conductor moves in a magnetic field, or the field changes in strength, and creates a flow of electricity.

insulate
To stop electricity by covering with a nonconducting material.

photovoltaic cell
A device that changes light energy directly into electrical energy, with no stages in between.

resistance
To oppose or act against the flow of electricity.